FIESTA!

Brazil

Charles Phillips

W
FRANKLIN WATTS
NEW YORK • LONDON • SYDNEY

First published 1998

Franklin Watts
96 Leonard Street
London EC2A 4RH

0 7496 2936 3

Dewey Decimal Classification Number: 394.2

A CIP catalogue record for this book is available from the British Library

Copyright © 1997 Marshall Cavendish Limited
119 Wardour Street, London W1V 3TD

Marshall Cavendish Limited
Editorial staff
Editorial Director: Ellen Dupont
Art Director: Joyce Mason
Designer: Trevor Vertigan
Sub-Editors: Susan Janes, Judy Fovargue
Production: Craig Chubb
Editorial Assistant: Lorien Kite

Crafts devised and created by Susan Moxley
Music arrangements by Harry Boteler
Photographs by Bruce Mackie
Translator and Consultant: Ana Fabres

Printed in Italy

Adult supervision advised for all crafts and recipes
particularly those involving sharp instruments and heat.

CONTENTS

BRAZIL

In eastern South America, Brazil is a huge country full of contrasts. Most people live near the coast.

Colombia **Venezue**

Japura

Jurua

Purus

Peru

▶ **Amazonia**, in western Brazil, is a wild jungle land. The Amazon River snakes through it.

▼ **Brasília**, the capital of Brazil, was built in just three years in the late 1950s.

▼ **Coffee** is an important crop. Brazil sells coffee to other countries. A legend tells that the first coffee beans were brought to Brazil from French Guiana by a soldier in the early 1700s.

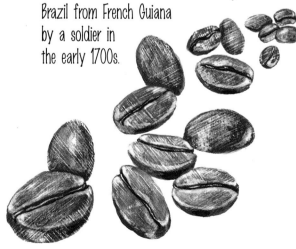

Surinam

French Guiana

Guyana

Macapá

Branco

Amazon

Negro

Belém

Manaus

Tocantins

Tapajos

Madeira

Recife

Xingu

Paraíba

São Francisco

Arinos

Araguaia

BRAZIL

Salvador

Bolivia

BRASILIA

Paraguay

Atlantic Ocean

Parana

Rio de Janeiro

São Paulo

Argentina

Porto Alegre

▶ **A statue** of Jesus Christ stands on top of Corcovado Mountain in the coastal city of Rio de Janeiro.

Uruguay

RELIGIONS

Christianity is the main faith in Brazil. But African religions are also popular. Some Brazilians go to Christian churches as well as to services of the African religions.

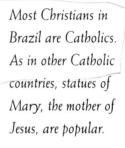

BRAZIL is the largest Roman Catholic country in the world. In Salvador, northeast Brazil, there are so many Catholic churches that you could go to a different one every day for a year.

The Portuguese settlers who came to Brazil in the 1600s were Catholics. The settlers brought slaves from Africa to harvest sugar cane on plantations in Brazil. Today in Brazil Catholicism and faiths that have grown from the religions of the slaves

Most Christians in Brazil are Catholics. As in other Catholic countries, statues of Mary, the mother of Jesus, are popular.

exist side by side. The main African cult is called "Candomblé" – or sometimes "Macumba". Candomblé is an African word that means "a dance to honour the gods". People who follow Candomblé say that you have a god, or *orixá*, who looks after you all through your life. There are many gods. Oxalá, the god of the sun, is the greatest. Oxúm is the god

Followers of the African religion Umbanda *wear these charms close to their hearts. They believe that the charms – decorated with gods' names – bring good luck.*

of fresh water. Iemanjá is the goddess of the sea. Candomblé priestesses and priests have a special custom. They throw seashells on the ground and can tell from the way the shells fall which of the gods is a person's orixá.

Some people think you can worship the Candomblé gods at the same time as praying to Jesus Christ or to Catholic saints. In the past Catholics tried to stop the slaves worshipping African gods because they wanted the slaves to learn the Catholic religion. The slaves became Catholics but also kept their old gods. The African gods were tied in to Catholicism. For example, people linked Oxalá to Jesus Christ. They also said that Iemanjá was like the Virgin Mary, mother of Jesus.

Umbanda, a version of Candomblé, is one of the most popular of the African religions. Its followers believe it is "white magic" – it can make good things happen, but not bad things.

GREETINGS FROM **BRAZIL!**

Brazil takes up almost half of South America. It is so big that it is winter at one end of the country when it is summer at the other end. There are many different people with their own ways of life. Gaúcho cowboys look after herds of cattle on huge grasslands in the far south of the country. Brazilian Indians live in wild jungles in the Amazon region in northwestern Brazil. Other people live in busy modern cities like São Paulo and Rio de Janeiro. The Indians have their own languages, but other Brazilians speak Portuguese.

How do you say...

Hello
Oí, olá or alô

Goodbye
Tchau

Thank you
Obrigado

Peace
Paz

FESTA DE IEMANJÁ

The feast of Iemanjá, an African goddess of the sea, is part of the New Year party in Rio de Janeiro, southeastern Brazil. People go to the beach to offer gifts to the goddess.

Iemanjá is a goddess of the African cult called Candomblé. The cult's priestesses wear long white robes and necklaces of glass beads. They mingle with the crowds on the Copacabana Beach in Rio. As darkness falls on December 31, they put lighted candles in the fine sands.

All the Candomblé gods and goddesses have favourite things. Everyone knows what Iemanjá likes. The people who come to the party bring her bottles of perfume, pieces of jewellery and fruit as presents. Some people simply throw the gifts into the waves. Others send them out to sea in wooden boats.

People in Salvador, northeast Brazil, hold parties for Iemanjá on February 2. Big crowds gather on the beach

Followers of Candomblé believe that Iemanjá (centre) is the mother of all the other gods and goddesses in their religion. They think she controls storms because she is the goddess of the sea. Sailors pray to Iemanjá for a safe voyage.

at Rio Vermelho. They can buy meat, fish or prawn snacks, cooked in spices and palm tree oil. Salvador is in Bahia state. Bahia is famous

for its food. On the beach drummers from the Candomblé temples play music, and the priestesses dance to it. People put their gifts for Iemanjá in baskets.

Priestesses load the baskets into fishing boats, and then fishermen sail the boats out into the deeper water. When they are far out to sea, the fishermen throw the baskets into the waves and look to see whether they sink or float. The baskets that sink are accepted by

the goddess. It is seen as a good sign. People believe she can make wishes come true.

The beach party lasts all day. The boats come back just before dark. All the people want to know if the baskets sank or not. Then people dance all night. Many of those at the beach party do not believe in Candomblé. But like people all over the world they are hoping for good luck in the year ahead.

Partygoers buy flowers and scatter the petals on the beach and in the waves on Iemanjá's feast day. They choose flowers in Iemanjá's favourite colours — white and pale blue.

In Rio tiny boats carrying gifts for Iemanjá are put into the sea. If the boats wash out to sea, it means that Iemanjá has accepted the presents and will grant the wishes of the person who brought them.

9

LAVAGEM DO BONFIM

The name of this festival means "the washing of Bonfim". Bonfim is a Catholic church in Salvador, northeast Brazil.

The Lavagem do Bonfim festival takes place on the second Thursday in January. It is a mix of Roman Catholicism and Candomblé, one of Brazil's African faiths. Candomblé priestesses and "novices" – girls who are training to be priestesses – get together early in the morning. They walk for five miles to the beautiful Bonfim Church in the suburbs of Salvador.

A procession forms behind them and follows them to the Church. Bands with electric guitars and drums play from the backs of trucks, and the people in the crowd dance as they go along.

A pretty square, lined with trees, stands in front of Bonfim

This doll's white robe is the traditional dress worn by women from Salvador. Around her wrist she wears the colourful ribbons sold to crowds at Lavagem do Bonfim. The plaster churchfront (top right) is a model of Bonfim Church.

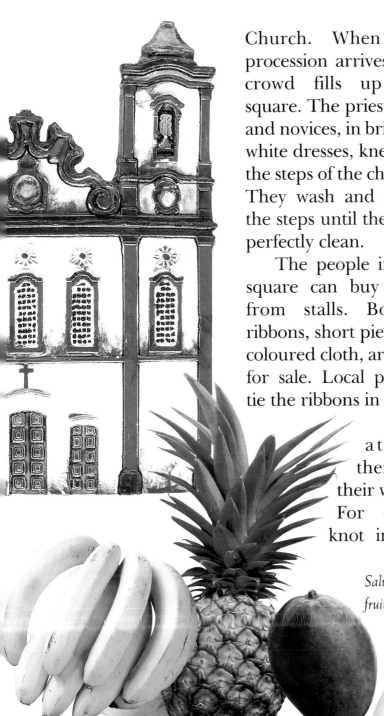

Church. When the procession arrives, the crowd fills up the square. The priestesses and novices, in brilliant white dresses, kneel on the steps of the church. They wash and scrub the steps until they are perfectly clean.

The people in the square can buy food from stalls. Bonfim ribbons, short pieces of coloured cloth, are also for sale. Local people tie the ribbons in knots and attach them to their wrists. For every knot in the ribbon they make a wish. Then they wear the ribbons on their wrists day after day, without ever taking them off. Eventually the ribbons fall off. When this happens, they believe, the wishes will come true. It is important not to buy the ribbon yourself. It must be a gift for the magic to work. People usually buy the ribbons and then give them to their friends.

Lights and flowers decorate the square. Music, dancing, eating and drinking go on for hours after the steps have been washed.

Salvador is known for its spicy cooking. Tropical fruits are common. Women in traditional white dresses sell food on the streets.

11

CARNIVAL

Carnival is a time of escape from day-to-day life. It has the reputation of being the best party in the world.

For a few days in either February or March the Brazilians forget their worries. Rich and poor mix together in a vast party. Brazilians look forward to Carnival all year round.

Normal rules do not apply at Carnival.

In Rio de Janeiro and other cities the mayor hands a large key to "Rei Momo", the fat king of Carnival. It stands for the key of the city and shows that Rei Momo will be in charge for the six days of the festival that lie ahead.

Thousands of people crowd into cities and towns, dancing, eating and drinking. Country people in the northeast part of Brazil walk to the towns and

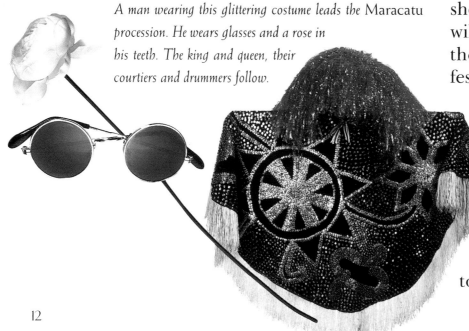

A man wearing this glittering costume leads the Maracatu procession. He wears glasses and a rose in his teeth. The king and queen, their courtiers and drummers follow.

The sun mask (above) and the bird mask (far left) are often worn in the "samba parade" – a procession of musicians and dancers that is one of the main attractions of Carnival. The white and purple mask (left) is worn by the woman dancer known as the flag bearer. She dances with a man, the dance master. Together they set the pace for the other dancers.

cities in the colourful *Maracatu* procession. This reminds them of the time when the Portuguese settlers would appoint a black ruler of the slaves for one year at a time. The procession is a coronation parade for a king and queen.

In the afternoons, musical bands playing drums and trumpets march the streets.

WHAT IS CARNIVAL?

Carnival began as a non-Christian festival in ancient Greece and Rome. Hundreds of years later it became linked to Christian celebrations. It takes place on the six days before Ash Wednesday, which is the first day of Lent, the period leading up to Easter. The Church expects Christians to give things up during Lent. The period of denial lasts until Easter, when Christians celebrate Jesus Christ rising from the dead. People began to see Carnival as a last chance to be merry before the plain meals and serious thoughts of Lent.

The Portuguese settlers brought Carnival customs with them to Brazil. Now the festival is less closely linked to its religious roots.

Children may wear plastic flower garlands (above) for Carnival. Throwing confetti and streamers (below) is a harmless way of making mischief.

People dance as they follow the bands. At night there are dances in private clubs, which are open to the public during Carnival. At these dances people wear bright costumes. Many also wear masks so that other people cannot tell who they are. This game of hiding who you really are is very old. People have worn carnival masks for hundreds of years – in Europe first, then in Brazil. At some clubs there are balconies built high up above the dance floor. People can stand here and throw streamers and confetti at the dancers below.

The parade of the samba schools is a major part of the Carnival. Huge crowds gather to watch them march past. The samba schools are not really schools but bands of musicians and dancers.

Each band chooses a theme for its show. The theme might be a folk tale or story from television. One year themes included the Amazon River, the history of the gypsies, and the story of coffee. In every school are hundreds of dancers and musicians. They wear costumes that tie in with the subject. They play a theme song for their show while they go by. Part of each school's show is a number of trucks carrying floats covered with statues and papier-mâché objects. The floats also tie in with the theme.

The samba parade takes place in the main avenue of the city. The organizers place tall benches down the sides of the avenue, and people sit on them to watch the fun. In Rio a special arena has been built just for the parade.

Anyone can join a samba school as a way of taking part in the carnival. But you have to be rich enough to pay for your own costume. And you have to be happy to go to the rehearsals for several months before the parade. People enjoy doing this. It makes the excitement of the Carnival last.

These drums, tambourines and other instruments are played by musicians in the percussion section of each samba school. They keep up a driving beat for the dancers. In the early days of Brazilian Carnival percussion instruments were made from bits of rubbish such as cans and bottletops.

AMAZON HEAD-DRESS

Carnival-goers often choose Amazon head-dresses when they are looking for unusual costumes. They base them on the feathered headwear worn by native Indians who live in the far west of Brazil.

Bright costumes are one of the most exciting parts of Brazilian Carnival. Each year in Rio de Janeiro a prize is awarded for the best costume worn at Carnival. Another prize goes to the samba school, or marching band, which puts on the best show in the samba school parade. When choosing the theme for their show, samba schools often decide on a Brazilian Indian legend or a subject connected with the Amazon rainforest.

The Brazilian Indians lived in Brazil long, long before the Portuguese settlers arrived in the early 1500s. Most now live in the Amazon region. They have very little contact with other Brazilians. There are some Indian tribes who have still never met anyone from outside the Amazon. In recent years people all over the world have become worried about damage to the Amazon rainforest and the Indians' way of life.

YOU WILL NEED
Paper
Knitting needles
PVA glue
Raffia
Beads
Feathers

1 Cut paper into strips about 5cm wide and 15cm long. Take a knitting needle and tuck one of the short edges of the strip around it. Roll the needle forward to make a cylinder 5cm tall. When you reach the end of the piece of paper, use glue to stick the end of the paper to the rest of the cylinder. Next sew the cylinders together side by side with raffia (above).

2 Take several small feathers, each about 5cm long. Insert one feather in the end of each paper cylinder in the row. Next take the beads and thread them onto three strips of raffia to make three small loops. Sew one loop at each end of the head-dress and one in the centre. Plait two lengths of raffia, each about 23cm long, for the ties. Tie the lengths to the bottom of the head-dress, one at each end. Finally, take a brightly coloured feather about 23cm long. Use a short piece of raffia to tie the feather in the middle of the head-dress (above).

FESTAS JUNINAS

Brazilians hold outdoor parties with huge bonfires, barbecued food, balloons, music and dancing to celebrate the "Festas Juninas", or June Festivals.

The days on which Roman Catholics remember the saints Anthony, Peter and John all come in June. In Brazil they are an excuse for a party. Saint Anthony's Day is June 12. Saint Peter's Day is June 28. But the most popular is the Feast of Saint John, which is on June 23 and 24.

The theme of the party on Saint John's Day is country life. Everyone dresses as a "country bumpkin" – a fool from down on the farm. Bands play country-style music. Families cook country food. One favourite is

On Saint John's Day people enjoy country dances like the square dance. The dancers go through set steps, following orders shouted by a master of ceremonies. They dress in brightly colored clothes made from cheap materials. This flowery cloth is used for mattress covers.

"pé-de-moleque" – a kind of peanut crunch. Some people pretend to be workers up from the country. They act out mock weddings on the streets, making the onlookers laugh.

In the evening huge bonfires light up the sky. In São Paulo, southern Brazil, a fire 21 metres tall is built and set alight each year. Paper balloons are an old custom for Saint John's Day. They are brightly decorated and sometimes filled with fireworks. A burning cloth is put inside them, and this lets off hot air that makes the balloon fly up high into the sky. But the balloons often catch fire and, when they fall, can start blazes on the ground. They have now been banned because they are so dangerous. These days

Children dress up in country style. Trousers with badly stitched patches in clashing colours are part of their outfit.

MAKES ABOUT 900G

600g sugar
350ml water
328g golden syrup
3 egg yolks, beaten
290g roasted peanuts,
coarsely chopped

PÉ-DE-MOLEQUE

1 You will need an adult to help you with this recipe. Lightly grease a shallow baking tin; leave aside.

2 Put sugar in a saucepan over low heat. Add water and stir until sugar dissolves. Stir in golden syrup.

3 Put a sugar thermometer in pan. Turn up heat and boil until mixture reaches 112° to 119°C. (This is when a drop of syrup will form a hard ball if dropped in ice-cold water.)

4 Carefully stir in egg yolks. Using a fork, twirl yolks around to make "threads". Stir in peanuts.

5 Carefully pour mixture into baking tin. Using a greased knife, mark into squares, but do not cut. Leave until cool and set.

6 To serve, cut into squares. Store any leftovers in an airtight tin to keep crisp.

RAINHA DE SÃO JOÃO

most people make do with ordinary blow-up balloons instead.

A traditional song for children to sing on Saint John's Day was "Cai cai balão" ("Fall, fall balloon"). The child in the song wants the beautiful burning balloon to fall into her hands. But her mother and father have told her she is not allowed to run after it and try to catch it, because she might be burned.

Families hang paper flags from posts around bonfires on Saint John's Day. Often a girl is elected Rainha de São João – Queen *of Saint John. She wears a crown and sash. Food like corn on the cob is cooked in the fires' embers.*

MAKING A MARACA

Songs and dancing are part of the fun at the Festas Juninas, as at many other Brazilian festivals. Children enjoy taking part in the music-making, sometimes using homemade instruments. The maraca is often made from a gourd, a type of fruit, that has been dried. It is filled with dried seeds that make a rattling sound when you shake the gourd.

CAI CAI BALÃO

cai cai ba-lão cai cai ba-lão a-

qui na min-ha mão não vou lá não vou lá não vou

lá ten-ho mo-do de ap-an-har

Fall, fall, balloon
Fall, fall balloon
Here, into my hand.

I won't go near it
I won't go near it
I won't go near it
Because I am afraid of being
burned.

1 Choose and blow up two small balloons. Glue strips of newspaper to them until they are covered all over. Hang them up to dry (left). Holding onto the end of the balloon sticking out from the stiff paper maraca, use a pin to burst the balloon. Remove the deflated balloon.

YOU WILL NEED
Balloons • Newspapers • PVA glue
Pin • Rice grains • Wooden handle
Tissue paper • Masking tape

3 Tear pieces of glitter paper and brightly coloured tissue paper into strips. Stick the strips on the maraca and the handle as decoration.

2 Pour rice grains through the hole where the end of the balloon was before. Attach wooden handle (below) to maraca using masking tape, positioning the handle over the hole.

21

FESTA DO 20 DE SETEMBRO

Each September 20 people in the far south of Brazil remember their history. The festival celebrates the customs of the Gaúchos who live in the area.

The state of Rio Grande do Sul in the far south of Brazil is the home of cowboys who look after huge herds of cattle. The cowboys are called "Gaúchos". But other people live there, too. Anyone who lives in Rio Grande do Sul is in fact a Gaúcho.

On September 20 the Gaúchos organize grand dances, or balls, with bands to play the dancers' favourite music. Before the ball they parade proudly around town on their fine horses.

People remember a famous revolt by the Gaúchos against the government of Brazil. On September 20, 1835, a man named

Gaúcho cowboys use leather lassos to control their cattle. They wear loose trousers, often in bright colours. Thick wool ponchos keep the cold out in winter.

22

Bento Gonçalves led a rebellion. He wanted Rio Grande to be a country separate from Brazil. This rebellion lasted ten years, but in the end the government beat Bento and his men. Local people honour the rebels once a year.

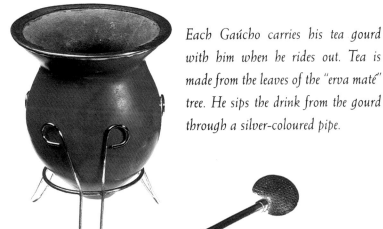

Each Gaúcho carries his tea gourd with him when he rides out. Tea is made from the leaves of the "erva maté" tree. He sips the drink from the gourd through a silver-coloured pipe.

SACI-PERERÊ

GAUCHOS TELL TALES of a small boy named Saci-Pererê who loves mischief. Saci lives on the "pampas", or grasslands, of Rio Grande do Sul. He waits in the undergrowth and then leaps out to play tricks on passersby. One night a cowboy named Eduardo was riding home. His horse, "Pingo", was tired. He paused at a crossroads.

Suddenly Pingo reared up on her hind legs. She squealed with fear. Eduardo turned in the saddle and caught a glimpse of an odd-looking little boy who had jumped on Pingo's back. The boy had only one leg. He was smoking a little pipe. Eduardo just had time to think, "Saci! You rascal!" Then Pingo was galloping away into the night.

NOSSA SENHORA DE APARECIDA

October 12 is a national holiday in Brazil to honour Nossa Senhora de Aparecida – "Our Lady of Aparecida". Catholic pilgrims come from far and wide to see a statue of Mary, the mother of Jesus. The statue made a miracle happen long ago.

ONE DAY in October 1717 the governor of São Paulo had to make a long trip across country. He took several servants and officers with him. In the middle of the day they came to a small village by the Paraiba River. The sun was hot. The governor wiped the sweat off his face with the back of his hand. He was tired and hungry, and so were his men.

At the side of the lane there was a cottage. "Enough is enough," the governor thought, "I will ask here for food." But the man who lived in the cottage was poor. He had no food, even for such an important visitor. He was a good man, however, and he offered to launch his boat on the river to try to catch fish to feed the governor.

The fisherman asked two friends to come along, and they hurried towards the river. The three men launched the boat on the water, which glittered in the sunshine. "This should be no trouble," the fisherman thought. "The river is always bountiful." But when the men pulled their nets in, they had caught only a few fish. There was not enough to feed one man, never mind a party.

The men flung out and hauled in their nets for a second time. This time there were no fish at all to be found in them. Instead, to their amazement, the men saw a statue, about 60cm tall, of a woman wearing a crown.

"It is our Lady," the first fisherman said, "Mary, the mother of Jesus." He bowed his head out of respect. Then he said, "Let us try just once more." This time when they pulled in the nets they were bulging with fish. They were so full that they almost burst as the men dragged them on board the boat.

"God be praised!" exclaimed the fisherman. "It is a miracle." There was plenty to feed the governor, his men – and all of the people in the village for many days. The story of how a statue of Our Lady from the sea performed a miracle was told many times over. Soon pilgrims were flocking to the village to see the statue.

CHRISTMAS

Brazilians celebrate the birth of Jesus with food and music. In the north of the country crowds in the streets dance the samba.

Christmas comes in the summertime for most of Brazil. But Brazilians keep many Christmas traditions from Europe, where Christmas falls in the winter. People put up Christmas trees in most Brazilian houses. "Papai Noel" – Santa Claus – wears a red suit with fur, just as he does in the United States and Europe.

Christmas is a time for family parties in Brazil. Aunts, uncles, parents and children share a big supper on Christmas Eve. People in northern Brazil often eat roast duck or pig at this meal. Turkey and baked ham are favourite dishes for Christmas supper in other parts of the country. *Rabanadas,*

Brazilian Catholics go to church at midnight on Christmas Eve after a family feast. At this meal they often sit for hours, drinking coffee and nibbling on nuts from a bowl.

which is rather like French toast, is served for dessert.

Later that night children put out their shoes near an open window. They hope that Papai Noel will climb in while they sleep and fill the shoes up with presents.

Nativity scenes are set up in many houses. Painted clay figures are laid out to tell the story of Jesus's birth in a stable.

RABANADAS

1 Heat oven on low setting. Cut bread in half diagonally, or use a pastry cutter to cut out rounds.
2 Put milk and 2 tbsp sugar in a large shallow bowl and stir. Add bread and soak 10 minutes.
3 Mix sugar, cinnamon and salt together in a bowl; leave aside.
4 Put egg whites in a clean bowl. Using an electric mixer, beat until they are thick and stand in stiff peaks when the beaters are lifted. Add egg yolks and beat again until thick.
5 Ask an adult to heat a few tablespoons of oil in a large frying pan over medium heat. Remove a slice of bread from milk and dip in eggs. Add to pan and fry until golden. Using a spatula, turn over. Continue frying until golden.
6 Drain on kitchen paper. Put on a plate and sprinkle with the cinnamon sugar. Keep warm in oven. Fry the remainder.

SERVES 4 – 6
8 slices white bread
900ml milk
2 tbsp plus 200g caster sugar
1 tbsp ground cinnamon
Pinch of salt
3 large eggs, separated
About 225ml vegetable oil

27

BUMBA-MEU-BOI

Actors in colourful costumes tell the tale of an ox that is killed but comes back to life. It is the main event in a street party that goes on all night.

Bumba-meu-boi means "whoa, my ox!" It is a play full of laughs and practical jokes but also touched with sadness. The play is put on in June in the northeast of Brazil, but in other areas it entertains the crowds at Christmas.

The play tells the story of a slave called Francis. His wife is about to have a baby. He steals and kills an ox in order to feed her. But he is caught. The farmer who owns the ox says that Francis must be killed unless he can bring the ox back to life. The farmer sends "the Captain" to tell Francis this. Now other slaves come to Francis's rescue. They ask some Brazilian Indians to make the ox better. The Indians use their magic to bring the ox back to life.

Crowds follow the actors through the streets to see the play. If members of the audience are hungry, they can buy food and drink from stands along the way. The play often starts in a church, where a priest washes the

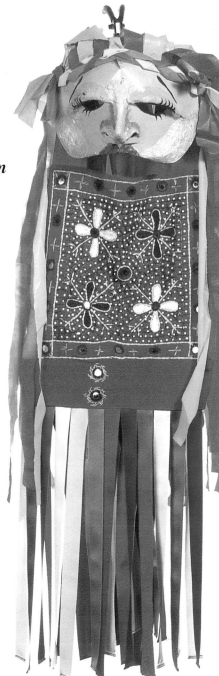

This mask and smock are a popular costume for the jokers who entertain the audience in Bumba-meu-boi. The Captain (left) wears a costume that makes him look as if he is on a donkey. He has to stop Francis getting away with the ox.

28

ox in holy water in a version of the service of baptism. One performer has to keep people in the crowd away from the actors. Sometimes the ox will disappear, and the other actors must run around looking for him. Then he will pop up unexpectedly.

Bumba-meu-boi began among the African slaves working on Brazilian sugar plantations in the 1700s. It was a way for the slaves to make fun of the plantation owners – the slaves win, while the farmer and the Captain look silly.

The actor who plays the ox, or "boi", wears a costume like this. It is a demanding part. The actor must be very fit because the ox performs several dances.

URRÕ URRÕ

ur - rõ ur - rõ ur - rõ ur -
rõ meu no - vil - ho bra - si - lei -
ro que a na - tu - re - za cri - ou São Jo -
ao Man - dou e pra mim fa -
zer é de min - ha ob - ri - ga -
cãs eu an - o - strar neu sa - bér

Urrõ urrõ is a favourite song in performances of Bumba-meu-boi.

Urrõ urrõ
Urrõ urrõ
My Brazilian calf
which Nature created
Saint John ordered
This is what I have to do
It is my duty
To tell the world about you.

OTHER IMPORTANT FESTIVALS

Colourful processions and ceremonies are at the heart of two country festivals in May and August.

In some towns two armies fight a mock battle on horseback as part of Festa do Divino.

FESTA DO DIVINO or Festival of the Holy Spirit is a Catholic festival. It is held at Pentecost, the day when God's Holy Spirit filled the first Christians 2,000 years ago. Groups of musicians tour the streets, playing religious songs. They visit each house they pass. The people in the houses give money or gifts. The money is used to pay for a big party. In some towns people dress in costumes and put on a mock battle between Christians and "Moors", or Arabs. It looks back to the time of the Crusades in the period 1000–1400, when Christians fought Arabs in what are now Palestine, Israel and Spain.

The Holy Spirit is usually seen as a dove. People think that the dove stands for peace.

The **FESTA DA SÃO ROQUE** takes place on August 16. Saint Roque is the spirit of a good dog. He is the patron saint of dogs. In the state of Amazonia, western Brazil, people put out food for dogs on Saint Roque's Day. They are happy to feed strays as well as pets. In other states they celebrate Saint Roque's Day with country dances.

Brazilian children are taught to pray to Saint Roque if they are scared of a big, fierce dog.

WORDS TO KNOW

Baptism: The ceremony in which someone is admitted into the Christian faith.

Candomblé: A cult that was brought to Brazil by African slaves. Candomblé means "a dance to honour the gods".

Cult: A group of people holding a set of religious beliefs; or the set of beliefs that they follow.

French toast: Bread dipped in a mixture of egg and milk and then fried.

Holy Spirit: Most Christians believe that God is three people: the Father, the Son and the Holy Spirit.

Lent: The forty days of fasting between Ash Wednesday and Easter.

Nativity: The birth of Jesus.

Patron saint: A saint who watches over a particular group. Nations, towns and professions all have patron saints.

Pentecost: A Christian festival, held seven weeks after Easter. At this time Christians celebrate the coming of the Holy Spirit.

Pilgrim: A person who makes a religious journey, or pilgrimage, to a holy place.

Rainforest: A dense tropical forest with very high rainfall. The Amazon rainforest in Brazil is the largest rainforest in the world.

Roman Catholic: A member of the Roman Catholic Church, the largest branch of Christianity. The head of this church is the Pope.

Saint: A title given to very holy people by some Christian churches. Saints are important in the Roman Catholic Church.

Samba: A lively, rythmic dance and the music that accompanies it.

Slave: A person who is, by law, owned by another person.

ACKNOWLEDGMENTS

WITH THANKS TO:

Rosandela and Sam Alexander , Acorda Porvo Brazilian Theatre Company, London. Chris Wells, percussionist. Maria das Graças Fish, Maggie Oswin and Everton Olivera, Brazilian Embassy, London. Flavio Souza and Loraine Schuch, London. The Chaia Silva family, Brasília. Ana Fabres, London. Fitch's Ark, The Animal Gallery, London.

PHOTOGRAPHS BY:

All photographs by Bruce Mackie except: John Elliott p19(bottom), p27(bottom). Cover photograph Puttkamer/ZEFA.

ILLUSTRATIONS BY:

Fiona Saunders title page, p4-5, Mountain High Maps ® Copyright © 1993 Digital Wisdom, Inc. p4-5. Tracy Rich p7. Philip Bannister p23. Alison Fleming p25.

INDEX